DON'T
FORGET TO
GO HOME

Never
Use
Pop Up
Windows

And 50 other
Ridiculous Web Rules

COLOPHON

BIS Publishers
Het Sieraad
Postjesweg 1
1057 DT Amsterdam
The Netherlands
T (+) 31 (0)20-515 02 30
F (+) 31 (0)20-515 02 39
bis@bispublishers.nl
www.bispublishers.nl

ISBN 978-90-6369-217-9

Ridiculous Design Rules is a concept developed
by Lemon Scented Tea and commissioned by
Premsela, Dutch Platform for Design and Fashion
(www.premsela.org).

Editorial Director: Anneloes van Gaalen
(www.paperdollwriting.com)
Designed by: Lilian van Dongen Torman
(www.born84.nl)

Printed in China.

BISPUBLISHERS

Never
Use
Pop Up
Windows

And 50 other
Ridiculous Web Rules

CONTENTS

'Never Use a PC', 'Never Use Copy Paste', 'Don't Forget the Attachment' and 'Don't Make Me Think'. Log on to a computer or go online and you're bound to come across one of these rules or any of the other 47 that are included in this book; rules that can serve as a guideline for gamers and a source of inspiration, or, in some cases, irritation for software developers. But don't think that only hardcore computer nerds will be able to relate to the rules compiled in this book. There's also plenty of web wisdom here that will appeal to even the most casual of surfers.

Besides rules governing web design, this book also features rules that come into play when communicating on the electronic highway. Think of the do's and don'ts when it comes to emailing and the netiquette that you need to stick to once you log on to any of the social media sites that crowd the web.

The quotes that accompany the rules either support or negate them. However, it's important to note that the aim in making this book was not to list all the rules that computer-loving individuals need to adhere to, neither did we want to decide which rules were indeed ridiculous and which were valuable words of wisdom. Instead, consider this book a source of comfort, joy and plain old fun, for PC lovers and Apple aficionados alike.

Also available in the Ridiculous Design Rules series are *Never Use White Type on a Black Background and 50 other Ridiculous Design Rules*, *Never Leave the House Naked and 50 other Ridiculous Fashion Rules*, and *The Medium is the Message and 50 other Ridiculous Advertising Rules*.

Never use a PC

It's the great PC vs Mac debate, as immortalized in an onslaught of Microsoft and Apple ads.

"Nobody messes with anyone in the tech industry the way Apple has messed with Microsoft. It's the first time I've ever seen a major national campaign that disparages a competitor, and the competitor just sits back and takes it."
Rob Enderle (1954), American technology analyst

"I'm a PC and I wear glasses."
Bill Gates (1955),
American businessman and
co-founder of Microsoft

"We've got cards and letters from lots of people that say iTunes is their favorite app on Windows. It's like giving a glass of ice water to somebody in hell."
Steve Jobs (1955),
American businessman and
co-founder of Apple and Pixar

"When we started working on [the Microsoft account] we swung everyone in the agency over to PCs, and really all of the senior people on the account are working on PCs, and we thought it was really important because we do a thing called method advertising, which is if you don't use it, you don't know how to talk about it. And I think in the past Microsoft's creative had a lot of swirly magical kind of stuff going on, and it might have been because their agencies weren't working on PCs. So once you start working on it and you understand you can do a better job on it, and I think we've done a really good job on it and, you know, one of the key factors is that we use them. I had never worked on a computer other than an Apple, and I thought, 'Oh my god! Will I be able to do this?'"
Alex Bogusky (1963), American advertising executive

"Microsoft isn't evil, they just make really crappy operating systems."
Linus Torvalds (1969), Finnish software engineer

DON'T FORGET TO GO HOME

ALWAYS MAKE THE TOP LEFT-HAND LOGO OF THE WEBSITE A HOME BUTTON

Consistency is key in the world of web usability. Most people do not react well to change. Those surfing the net are no exception.

"Ever since Google has become a verb, people have been using websites differently. Home pages aren't important any more. You search for what you are searching for and you will appear somewhere. The home page is now almost like the cover of a book. It's there, but it's not what you read. It's becoming much, much more important to design deep, deep web pages. It's important that you can find a complete hierarchy and that you know where you are. In old-fashioned websites, you would have a home page and if you went deep you could never get back - you never knew where you were, but that wouldn't matter, you went down then you went out. Now, no matter where you are, you can go in any direction. It means that clutter will make it worse and sites will have to be designed a little more tidily."
Erik Spiekermann (1947), German typographer and designer

"Keep the navigation in the same place on every page, so I don't have to go looking for it."
Steve Krug (1950), American writer and usability consultant

"Consistency is one of the most powerful usability principles: when things always behave the same, users don't have to worry about what will happen. Instead, they know what will happen based on earlier experience. Every time you release an apple over Sir Isaac Newton, it will drop on his head. That's good."
Jakob Nielsen (1957), Danish usability consultant

Always use
landscape
format
pictures in
web design

RULE
03

Thanks to a little thing called rotating computer screens, the landscape format picture rule no longer applies.

———————

"Most printed pieces – books, magazines, brochures, newspapers – are in portrait format, i.e., they are taller than wide. As computer monitors are wider than tall, web pages also have to be in landscape format."
Erik Spiekermann (1947), German typographer and designer

Surfers don't read

This may hurt the copywriter that gets paid by the word, but websites aren't read, they are scanned. So the less text, the better.

"One of the very few well-documented facts about web use is that people tend to spend very little time reading most web pages. Instead, we scan (or skim) them, looking for words or phrases that catch our eye. The exception, of course, is pages that contain documents like news stories, reports, or product descriptions. But even then, if the document is longer than a few paragraphs, we're likely to print it out – since it's easier and faster to read on paper than on a screen."
Steve Krug (1950), American author and usability consultant

"People rarely read web pages word by word; instead, they scan the page, picking out individual words and sentences. In research on how people read websites we found that 79 percent of our test users always scanned any new page they came across; only 16 percent read word-by-word."
Jakob Nielsen (1957), Danish usability consultant

"Everyone who's observed, tested, or studied online reading agrees that people behave differently when online. When viewing a new page, they don't read – they scan. They look at headings and subheadings first; they scan for hyperlinks, numerals, and keywords. They jump around, scrolling and clicking – their fingers never far from the browser's 'Back' button. The word that best describes their behavior is: impatient."
Gerry McGovern (1962), Irish content management expert

NEVER
TUPE
IN ALL
CAPS

RULE
05

You're excited, we get it. An exclamation point gets that same message across, so there is absolutely no need to go all caps on us.

———————

"If you really want to aggravate someone, using all caps is an effective way to do it. A study of email users in the United States and Britain found that overuse of capitals was the thing that most irritated email recipients."
David Shipley and Will Schwalbe, American authors of Send: The Essential Guide to Email for Office and Home *(2007)*

"Do not forgo the liberal use of capitals within your text, for the geometric letter forms can provide some diabolically good outcomes."
Paul Felton, graphic designer and author of The Ten Commandments of Typography *(2006)*

"Perpetrators of proper crimes against linguistics should be tried, convicted and locked inside a dusty, moth-ridden library with a set of dictionaries until they start coming out with proper sentences again. After rehabilitation, an alarm should go off when they touch caps lock, while a colon and bracket pressed in quick succession should delete all the text they'd previously written."
Ariane Sherine (1980), British comedy writer and journalist

Lose the smiley

RULE
06

They pop up in emails, text messages and in web forums: emoticons. There's some debate about who came up with the digital smiley face. Scott Fahlman usually gets the credit, for it was this American professor of computer science who – on September 19, 1982 – wrote a post in which he suggested the use of the ☺ to make clear to one and all that something has been written in jest. Fahlman: "The smiley idea may have appeared and disappeared a few times before my 1982 post. I probably was not the first person ever to type these three letters in sequence, perhaps even with the meaning of 'I'm just kidding' and perhaps even online. But I do believe that my 1982 suggestion was the one that finally took hold, spread around the world, and spawned thousands of variations."

"Q: How do you rank yourself among writers (living) and of the immediate past?
Nabokov: I often think there should exist a special typographical sign for a smile – some sort of concave mark, a supine round bracket, which I would now like to trace in reply to your question."
Vladimir Nabokov (1899-1977),
Russian-American author

*"The computer can't tell you the emotional story.
It can give you the exact mathematical design, but
what's missing is the eyebrows."*

Frank Zappa (1940-1993), American musician

19-Sep-82 11:44 Scott E Fahlman :-)
From: Scott E Fahlman <Fahlman at
Cmu-20c>
I propose that the following character
sequence for joke markers: :-) Read it
sideways. Actually, it is probably more
economical to mark things that are
NOT jokes, given current trends. For
this, use :-(
*Scott Fahlman (1948), American
professor of computer science*

"Emoticons are lame, kitschy, and
annoying. But worst of all they're
ineffective. Think about it: The range
of human emotions is enormous and
complex. The existing library of emoticons is not. I mean, how do you express
feelings of cautious optimism with a
few dots and a squiggle?"
*Daniel Dumas (1981), American
journalist for Wired*

"The emoticon is so damn needy.
The smiley is the rimshot of online
communication (which makes the
frowny the sad trombone). It clings
to your virtual leg, begging for your
approval. 'Love me!' it says. 'Understand me! I am trivial and light of
heart even when in despair!'"
*Mary Elizabeth Williams, American
journalist*

"The addition of an emoticon doesn't
guarantee that there won't be hurt
feelings."
*David Shipley and Will Schwalbe,
American authors of* Send: The
Essential Guide to Email for Office
and Home *(2007)*

RULE 06	RULE 06	RULE 06	RULE 06	RULE 06	RULE 06	RULE 06
RULE 06	RULE 06	RULE 06	RULE 06	RULE 06	RULE 06	RULE 06
RULE 06	RULE 06	RULE 06	RULE 06		RULE 06	RULE 06
RULE 06	RULE 06	RULE 06	RULE 06	RULE 06	RULE 06	RULE 06
RULE 06	RULE 06	RULE 06	RULE 06	RULE 06	RULE 06	RULE 06
RULE 06	RULE 06	RULE 06	RULE 06	RULE 06	RULE 06	RULE 06
RULE 06	RULE 06	RULE 06	RULE 06	RULE 06	RULE 06	RULE 06
RULE 06	RULE 06	RULE 06	RULE 06	RULE 06	RULE 06	RULE 06
RULE 06	RULE 06	RULE 06	RULE 06	RULE 06	RULE 06	RULE 06
RULE 06	RULE 06	RULE 06	RULE 06	RULE 06	RULE 06	RULE 06

PLAY NICE!

It's like your mother used to say: if you don't have anything nice to say, don't say anything at all. When blogging, tweeting or emailing: play nice.

"It was easier for me when I was coming up, there was no such thing as the 24/7 news cycle. For younger actresses, the scrutiny is very hard. The blogosphere where people comment on their weight, their appearance, endlessly. That always happened but it happened in apartments and restaurants. You didn't hear everybody's opinion of you [all the time]."
Meryl Streep (1949), American actress

"I definitely don't read anything: I don't read blogs, don't surf the web, don't look for comments on myself, don't Google myself – never have never will. But I can't really pay attention to all the chat about me – that may or may not exist, positive or negative. I just don't see that that's really a valuable use of my time."
Sarah Jessica Parker (1965), American actress

"Whether you like me or not, I'm not going away anytime soon. I don't care if you like me, I just care if you read my website."
Mario Armando Lavandeira, aka Perez Hilton (1978), American celebrity blogger

Develop for multiple browsers

If you can't come up with a one-size-fits-all design, then be sure you develop for multiple browsers. It's only right.

───────────

"Anyone who slaps a 'this page is best viewed with Browser X' label on a web page appears to be yearning for the bad old days, before the web, when you had very little chance of reading a document written on another computer, another word processor, or another network."
Tim Berners-Lee (1955), British engineer, often credited as the inventor of the World Wide Web

Illegal downloading is like masturbation (everybody does it)

RULE
09

Illegal downloading is similar to masturbation. It's a largely solitary, albeit pleasurable, undertaking. And while everybody does it, only few are willing to admit to doing it.

"Forbid a man to think for himself or to act for himself and you may add the joy of piracy and the zest of smuggling to his life."
Elbert Hubbard (1856-1915), American publisher and writer

"I have no emotional connection to money. And somehow I became the greedy Danish drummer, because of this Napster thing. Give away stuff for free? Not a problem. The Internet? Not a problem... Who makes the decision? We make the decision. I'll give away all my shit for free. But I'll decide when and where and how."
Lars Ulrich (1963), Danish drummer of Metallica known for taking on Napster

"I don't mind people stealing my music. That's fine. But I think they should steal everything. You know how much money the oil companies have? If you need some gas, just go fill your tank off and drive off, they're not going to miss it."
Kid Rock (1971), American singer

MAKE YOUR SITE EASY TO NAVIGATE

RULE
10

The last thing you want is for your visitors to feel lost. Improve site navigation and people will feel right at home ...

———

"Design is the conscious effort to impose a meaningful order."
Victor Papanek (1927-1999),
Austrian designer

"We're inherently lost when we're on the web, and we can't peek over the aisles to see where we are. web navigation compensates for this missing sense of place by embodying the site's hierarchy, creating a sense of 'there'. Navigation isn't just a feature of a website; it is the website... The moral? Web navigation had better be good."
Steve Krug (1950), American author and usability consultant

"Good web navigation design is not about giving people lots and lots of choices. It is not about second guessing decisions we have made. It's not about asking what if we want to get back to where we were. It's about looking forward, not about looking backward."
Gerry McGovern (1962), Irish content management expert

TREAT YOUR PASSWORD
LIKE YOUR TOOTHBRUSH

To quote American author Clifford Stoll (1951): "Treat your password like your toothbrush. Don't let anybody else use it, and get a new one every six months."

"Usability suffers when users type in passwords and the only feedback they get is a row of bullets. Typically, masking passwords doesn't even increase security, but it does cost you business due to login failures."
Jakob Nielsen (1957), Danish usability consultant

"What's your password? You don't have to answer that. Is it 'gates'? (...) Did you ever have a pet when you were younger? What was the pet's name?"
Jon Stewart (1962), American comedian and host of 'The Daily Show' interviewing Bill Gates

"Passwords are like underwear: you don't let people see it, you should change it very often, and you shouldn't share it with strangers."
Chris Pirillo (1973), American writer and tech expert

"Back at the dawn of the web, the most popular account password was '12345.' Today, it's one digit longer but hardly safer: '123456'. According to a new analysis, one out of five web users still decides to leave the digital 'equivalent of a key under the doormat: they choose a simple, easily guessed password like 'abc123', 'iloveyou' or even 'password' to protect their data."
Ashlee Vance, author of "If Your Password is 123456, Just Make It HackMe", New York Times article (2010)

Use a grid

The grid has long been a staple in the toolbox of designers and graphic artists alike, providing the framework and underlying structure for their designs. But as Mark Boulton, author of *Designing Grid Systems for the Web*, points out, when designing for the web, you and your grids had better be flexible: "Good designers for the web know that the users who use their sites ... have the power to change things. The designer has lost, to a degree, the ability to control.... We can't be upset when the user wants to change something like the text size. What we can do is design grid systems to adapt to those changes."

"A design should have some tension and some expression in itself. I like to compare it with the lines on a football field. It is a strict grid. In this grid you play a game and these can be nice games or very boring games."
Wim 'Gridnik' Crouwel (1928), Dutch graphic designer and typographer

"Grids are very handy, but should never be an end in itself."
Robin Uleman (1969), Dutch graphic designer

"Grid Systems have been used in print design, architecture and interior design for generations. Now, with the advent of the World Wide Web, the same rules of grid system composition and usage no longer apply. Content is viewed in many ways; from RSS feeds, to email. Content is viewed on many devices; from mobile phones to laptops. Users can manipulate the browser, they can remove content, resize the canvas, resize the typefaces. A designer is no longer in control of this presentation."
Mark Boulton (1973), British graphic designer

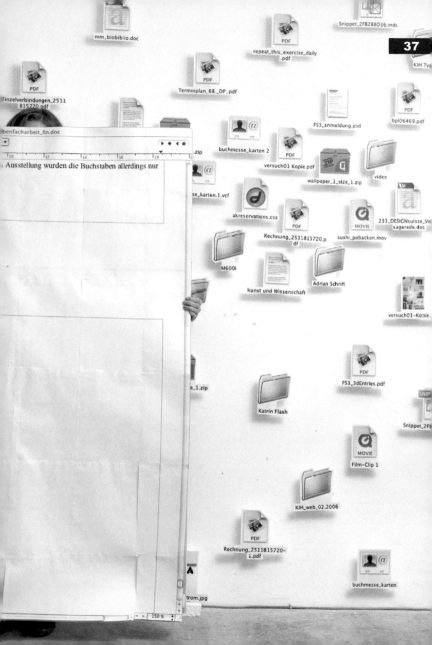

Pretty is nice but content comes first

It's easy to get lost in the details, but a well-designed website with bad or little content or a beautiful-looking game with little to no gameplay is just not okay. Content should always come first.

———

"I feel that people like Mario and people like Link and the other characters we've created not for the characters themselves, but because the games they appear in are fun. Because people enjoy playing those games first, they come to love the characters as well."
Shigeru Miyamoto (1952), Japanese game designer

"We made the buttons on the screen look so good you'll want to lick them."
Steve Jobs (1955), American businessman, co-founder of Apple and Pixar

"Web users ultimately want to get at data quickly and easily. They don't care as much about attractive sites and pretty design."
Tim Berners-Lee (1955), British engineer, often credited as the inventor of the World Wide Web

"Environments in computer games are getting more and more real, and now the power of the new machines allows us to create very complex physics and maths engines. But we mustn't be distracted from the main focus of game development – gameplay environments can only ever play a supporting role to gameplay, just as cool graphics do."
Peter Molyneux (1959), British game designer

Good design solves the right problem

In his 2002 essay "Taste for Makers", programmer-turned-author Paul Graham (1964) listed his personal principles of design. Graham, who founded the first ASP (application service provider), believes good design is simple, hard, timeless, suggestive, often slightly funny, looks easy, uses symmetry, resembles nature and solves the right problem.

"Design is a problem-solving activity."
Paul Rand (1914-1996), American graphic designer

"Of course design is about problem solving, but I cannot resist adding something personal."
Wim Crouwel (1928), Dutch graphic designer and typographer

"The computer was born to solve problems that did not exist before."
Bill Gates (1955), American businessman and co-founder of Microsoft

"The thing that has always driven me as a designer is feeling pissed off by the shitty stuff around me and wanting to make it better."
Marc Newson (1963), Australian designer

"The best programmers are not marginally better than merely good ones. They are an order-of-magnitude better, measured by whatever standard: conceptual creativity, speed, ingenuity of design, or problem-solving ability."
Randall Stross, American author

Don't forget the 404 error page

Leave it to Danish usability expert Jakob Nielsen to point out that the 404 error page, which is often overlooked by designers, could in fact serve as a useful teaching tool. "The most common guideline violation is when an error message simply says something is wrong, without explaining why and how the user can fix the problem. Such messages leave users stranded. Informative error messages not only help users fix their current problems, they can also serve as a teachable moment."

—————

"If you actually do enough user testing, you'll be able to spare me from many errors before they happen. But where the potential for error is unavoidable, always provide a graceful, obvious way for me to recover."
Steve Krug (1950), American author and usability consultant

"Error messages are a special form of feedback: they tell users that something has gone wrong... Typically, users won't invest time in reading and learning about features, but they will spend the time to understand an error situation if you explain it clearly, because they want to overcome the error."
Jakob Nielsen (1957), Danish usability consultant

"Never settle for the default 404 page. Replace it with a custom 404 page that is polite, illuminating, and most of all, helpful."
Jeff Atwood (1970), American software developer

404 error: File not found

HTTP standard

01110111 01110010 01101001 01110100 01100101 00100000 01111001 01101111
01110101 01110010 00100000 01101111 01110111 01101110 00100000 01100011
01101111 01100100 01100101 01110111 01110010 01101001 01110100 01100101
00100000 01111001 01101111 01110101 01110010 00100000 01101111 01110111
01101110 00100000 01100011 01101111 01100100 01100101 01110111 01110010
01101001 01110100 01100101 00100000 01111001 01101111 01110101 01110010
00100000 01101111 01110111 01101110 00100000 01100011 01101111 01100100
01100101 01110111 01110010 01101001 01110100 01100101 00100000 01111001
01101111 01110101 01110010 00100000 01101111 01110111 01101110 00100000
01100011 01101111 01100100 01100101 01110111 01110010 01101001 01110100
01100101 00100000 01111001 01101111 01110101 01110010 00100000 01101111
01110111 01101110 00100000 01100011 01101111 01100100 01100101 01110111
01110010 01101001 01110100 01100101 00100000 01111001 01101111 01110101
01110010 00100000 01101111 01110111 01101110 00100000 01100011 01101111
01100100 01100101 01110111 01110010 01101001 01110100 01100101 00100000
01111001 01101111 01110101 01110010 00100000 01101111 01110111 01101110
00100000 01100011 01101111 01100100 01100101 01110111 01110010 01101001
01110100 01100101 00100000 01111001 01101111 01110101 01110010 00100000
01101111 01110111 01101110 00100000 01100011 01101111 01100100 01100101
01110111 01110010 01101001 01110100 01100101 00100000 01111001 01101111
01110101 01110010 00100000 01101111 01110111 01101110 00100000 01100011
01101111 01100100 01100101 01110111 01110010 01101001 01110100 01100101
00100000 01111001 01101111 01110101 01110010 00100000 01101111 01110111
01101110 00100000 01100011 01101111 01100100 01100101 01110111 01110010
01101001 01110100 01100101 00100000 01111001 01101111 01110101 01110010
00100000 01101111 01110111 01101110 00100000 01100011 01101111 01100100
01100101 01110111 01110010 01101001 01110100 01100101 00100000 01111001
01101111 01110101 01110010 00100000 01101111 01110111 01101110 00100000
00100000 01101111 01110111 01101110 00100000 01100011 01101111 01100100
01100101 01110111 01110010 01101001 01110100 01100101 00100000 01111001
01101111 01110101 01110010 00100000 01101111 01110111 01101110 00100000
01100011 01101111 01100100 01100101 01110111 01110010 01101001 01110100
01100101 00100000 01111001 01101111 01110101 01110010 00100000 01101111
01110111 01101110 00100000 01100011 01101111 01100100 01100101 01110111

01101111 01110111 01101110 00100000 01100011 01101111 01100100 01100101
01110111 01110010 01101001 01110100 01100101 00100000 01111001 01101111
01110101 01110010 00100000 01101111 01110111 01101110 00100000 01100011
01101111 01100100 01100101 01110111 01110010 01101001 01110100 01100101
00100000 01111001 01101111 01110101 01110010 00100000 01101111 01110111
01101110 00100000 01100011 01101111 01100100 01100101 01110111 01110010
01101001 01110100 01100101 00100000 01111001 01101111 01110101 01110010
00100000 01101111 01110111 01101110 00100000 011000 **RULE** 11 01100100
01100101 01110111 01110010 01101001 01110100 011001 **1б** 00 01111001
01101111 01110101 01110010 00100000 01101111 01110111 0101110 00100000

Write your own code

01100011 01101111 01100100 01100101 01110111 01110010 01101001 01110100
01100101 00100000 01111001 01101111 01110101 01110010 00100000 01101111
01110111 01101110 00100000 01100011 01101111 01100100 01100101 01110111
01110010 01101001 01110100 01100101 00100000 01111001 01101111 01110101

01110111 01110010 01101001
01110100 01100101 00100000
01111001 01101111 01110101
01110010 00100000 01101111
01110111 01101110 00100000
01100011 01101111 01100100
01100101

"It's OK to figure out murder mysteries, but you shouldn't need to figure out code. You should be able to read it."
Steve McConnell, American author of Code Complete *(1993, 2004)*

"Writing code has a place in the human hierarchy worth somewhere above grave robbing and beneath managing."
Gerald Weinberg (1933), American computer scientist

"Good code is its own best documentation."
Steve McConnell, American software author

"Any code of your own that you haven't looked at for six or more months might as well have been written by someone else."
Eagleson's Law of Programming

never use copy and paste

Never in the history of man has it been so easy to copy and paste somebody else's work. A couple of basic keyboard shortcuts – Ctrl+C and Ctrl+V – have turned plagiarism into child's play.

"If an innovative piece of software comes along, Microsoft copies it and makes it part of Windows. This is not innovation. This is the end of innovation."
Larry Ellison (1944), American businessman, co-founder and CEO of Oracle

"I cannot see how copying things from the internet and passing them off as your own can be seen other than seriously. Virtually everywhere in the world, plagiarism by students at schools and universities is on the increase, whether in writing an application form or in filling essays or theses with information directly lifted from Wikipedia or Google... The fault lies with the internet. Yes, cheating has always been around in schools and universities, but never before on such an industrial and technological scale. The easy access provided by the internet is a direct threat to individual and original thinking, writing and scholarship."
Marcel Berlins (1941), French-born British lawyer and columnist

"Use your fucking brain. People don't think enough. People don't use their brain. They use copy-paste. Your brain is free. It is fast. Wickedly fast."
Erik Spiekermann (1947), German typographer and designer

"How can we ever find an individual signature in this copy culture."
Geert Lovink (1959), Dutch media theorist

"We rip, steal, burn, cut and paste. Reproduction is the essence of successful design."
Hendrik-Jan Grievink (1977), Dutch editorial designer

All good design is done by Photoshop

All good design might be done by Photoshop, but as Stephen Newberry, Technical Resources Manager at Adobe Systems Europe, points out, "A camera does not make a photographer; Photoshop does not make a designer."

———

"Photoshop is useful in many ways, but must NEVER be used for the altering of photographs. My assistants and my agency do whatever Photoshop work for me that may be required as it is too complicated for my brain."
Elliott Erwitt (1928), French-born American photographer

"A lot of clients assume you can do things with Photoshop [which often you can't]. They say, 'Oh, we've just changed this product color, can you change the color in the photograph?' Sometimes clients want you to do something in Photoshop because they have this vague idea that everything's easy."
David Pearce (1948), London agency Tatham Pearce

"Photoshop is a tool and it's driven by the person behind it, so it's their creativity that's being enhanced by it. There are many misconceptions about it and how easy it is."
Otto Greenslade, British visual and interaction designer

DON'T MAKE ME THINK!

According to Steve Krug, author of *Don't Make Me Think: A Common Sense Approach to Web Usability*, the above-mentioned rule is the first law of usability: "It's the overriding principle – the ultimate tie breaker when deciding whether something works or doesn't in a web design. If you have room in your head for only one usability rule, make this the one."

"Think? Why think! We have computers to do that for us."
Jean Rostand (1894-1977), French biologist, writer and philosopher

"What users want is convenience and results."
Jef Raskin (1943-2005), American human-computer interface expert

"The 'law' itself is pretty simple: Don't make me think. I've used it for years with my clients, and it really means exactly what it says: Don't do things that force people to think unnecessarily when they're using your site. I find that most people are quite willing and able to think when it's necessary, but making them do it when there's nothing in it for them (other than compensating for your failure to sort things out properly) tends to be annoying – and worse, confusing."
Steve Krug (1950), American author and usability consultant

"Email programs have to remove that 'Reply All' button farther away from the 'Reply' button."

In his TV show, *Real Time*, American comedian Bill Maher warned against placing the 'Reply' button next to the 'Reply All' button: "It's too dangerous. It's the computer equivalent of the vagina being so close to the sphincter. Just because God made a horrible mistake doesn't mean Microsoft has to."

"To err is human – and to blame it on a computer is even more so."
Robert Orben (1927), American magician and comedy writer

"Most people think of their inbox as some sort of virginal property that must be protected from unsolicited advances. And they can quickly turn against you if they think that you are somehow responsible for sullying that sanctity. One way that happens very quickly is if you send a message out to a bunch of people wherein everyone's email address is visible in the To: or CC: line. That invites potentially annoying 'Reply-Alls' from unsavvy folks who mean to just be replying to you, followed by another round of 'Reply Alls' from people asking not to be included in 'Reply Alls'."
David Goldenberg (1979), American journalist

Get

Tested

You can build or design a great website, kick-ass game or downright brilliant software program, but the proof is in the pudding. Testing the program, system or service before take-off is a sure way of finding and fixing faults. After that it's pretty much all systems go.

"Supposing is good, but finding out is better."
Mark Twain, aka Samuel Clemens (1835-1910), American author

"Testing shows the presence, not the absence of bugs."
Edsger W. Dijkstra (1930-2002), Dutch computer scientist

"All of the theory in the world, and the wisest guru, cannot always predict how an interface will work in practice. One must test, objectively observe, and modify the interface if testing shows that users have difficulties. It is never the user's fault, but also remember that people find it difficult to change, so difficulties based on previous habits may not be dispositive."
Jef Raskin (1943-2005), American human-computer interface expert

"Usability testing should be very simple. It just means sitting down and watching somebody who's not you try and use the thing you're building."
Steve Krug (1950), American author and usability consultant

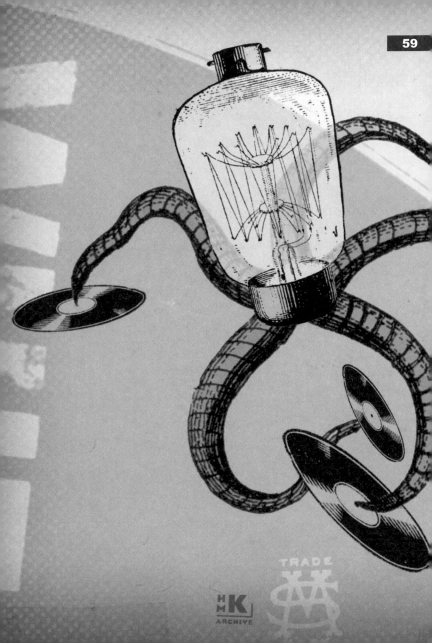

"Here are the main things I know
about testing: If you want a great site,
you've got to test... Testing one user is
100 percent better than testing none...
Testing one user early in the project is
better than testing 50 near the end...
The point of testing is not to prove or
disprove something. It's to inform your
judgment... Testing isn't something
you do once. You make something, test
it, fix it and test it again..."
*Steve Krug (1950), American author
and usability consultant*

"Software testing. It is exhilarating.
It is exasperating. It can be the best
of jobs – or the worst. It is fundamental
to delivering quality software on time
within budget."
Edward Kit, author of Software
Testing in the Real World *(1995)*

**"I'm not saying we purposely introduced bugs
or anything, but this is kind of a natural result of any
complexities of software, that you can't fully test it."**

Will Wright (1960), American video game designer

Leave them wanting more

You want your game to be addictive and your website to be a place people want to visit again and again and again.

"Leave them wanting more and you know they'll call you back."
Bobby Womack (1944), American musician

"The perfect game, in my mind, is one that you can play within fifteen seconds but enjoy playing for ten minutes or ten hours."
Peter Molyneux (1959), British game designer

"The ultimate test of a game's worth occurs as soon as the game ends: if the players genuinely and unhesitatingly want to play more, you've got a winner. If not, then go back into your game design cave and tinker with your design some more."
Andrew J. Looney (1963), American game designer

"Puzzle games are the most addictive games there are. I could compete against myself for higher and higher scores. I think that puzzle games are far less boring than other games, because their major strength is their gameplay, which makes up for their lack of graphics and gimmicks."
Demis Hassabis (1976), British game designer

SCORE
004383

LEVEL
02

LINES
33

NEXT

Never write an email while you are angry

An old Chinese proverb says that you should never write a letter when you're angry. The means of communication might have changed, but these words of wisdom still ring true today. So keep your emotions in check and if you are going to write an email while you're angry, at least think twice before hitting the send button.

———

"Never write a letter while you are angry."
Chinese Proverb

"If we are typing while agitated, the absence of information on how the other person is responding makes the prefrontal circuitry for discretion more likely to fail. Our emotional impulses disinhibited, we type some infelicitous message and hit 'send' before a more sober second thought leads us to hit 'discard'. We flame."
Daniel Goleman (1946), American psychologist

"I don't believe in email. I'm an old-fashioned girl. I prefer calling and hanging up."

Carrie Bradshaw,
aka Sarah Jessica Parker (1965),
American actress

"The age of technology has both re-vived the use of writing and provided ever more reasons for its spiritual solace. Emails are letters, after all, more lasting than phone calls, even if many of them r 2 cursory 4 u."
Anna Quindlen (1952), American
author and journalist

"The speed of email doesn't just make it easier to lose our cool – it actually eggs us on. On email, people aren't quite themselves: they are angrier, less sympathetic, less aware, more easily wounded, even more gossipy and duplicitous. Email has a tendency to encourage the lesser angels of our nature."
David Shipley and Will Schwalbe,
American authors of Send: The Essential Guide to Email for Office and Home *(2007)*

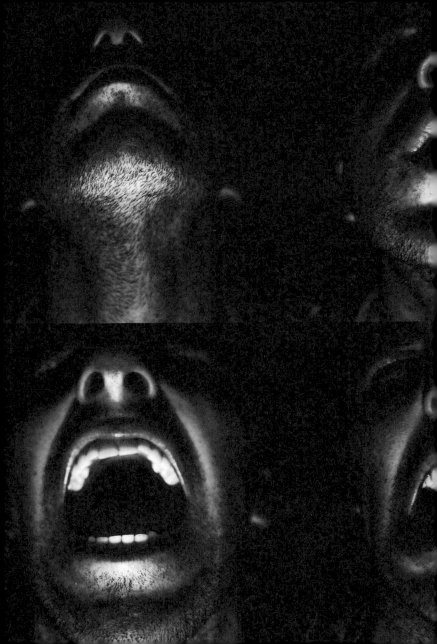

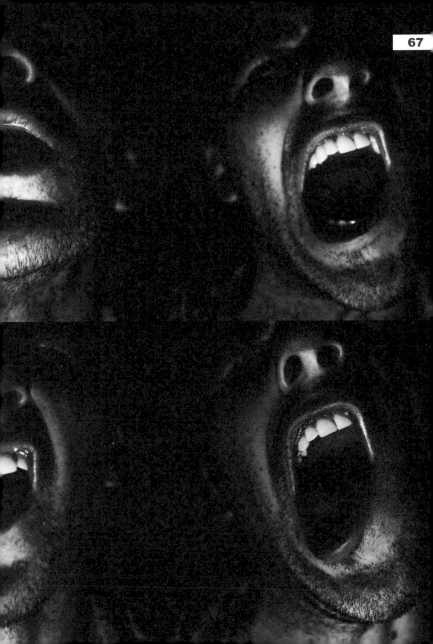

ACCEPT ALL FACEBOOK FRIEND REQUESTS

To accept or decline, that is the question.
Facebook users face this dilemma every
time they receive a friend request. It
might be tempting to accept one and all,
but do you really want your boss or
ex-lover to see your personal photos
or read your updates?

FACEBOOK
IS MORE
ADDICTIVE
THAN
CRACK.

"Some people adopt an everyone-welcome policy on Facebook and accept all friend requests; some only want real-world contacts in their friends list. In deciding on the right approach for you, bear in mind that the bigger your friend network is, the more application, event, chat session and cause invitations you'll receive – and that can lead to some uncomfortable moments and the occasional friend purge."
Christopher Null (1971), American entertainment and technology writer

"If you've been on Facebook for more than a week, you've probably gotten a friend request from someone you don't know, someone you hate, or someone you don't want snooping around your profile… Most of you will hold your nose and accept the request. But why? This is like allowing a corsair-wielding pirate to board your vessel without a fight. Once you've accepted too many faux friends, Facebook becomes a real slog."
Reihan Salam (1979), Bangladeshi-American writer and journalist

"'Defriending', or ostracizing a former pal from one's digital inner circle, might seem to be the pinnacle of linguistic modernity. When the act of defriending was first committed is perhaps lost forever in the fog of history. Surely this historic moment did not take place in 17th-century Holland? Perhaps it did, as Dutch writer Ed Schilders has found. Using the tried and true technique of lexicographical research (i.e. looking something up in the dictionary), he discovered the Dutch translation of the word, *ontvriending*, dates back to at least 1626. He found the term in *De Woordenboek der Nederlandsche Taal*, an exhaustive 43-volume opus on the Dutch language, which took more than a century to complete."
NRC Handelsblad (*Dutch newspaper*), *January 15, 2010*

Always create a backup copy

Back up or shut up. You didn't create
any backup copies? Take the loss like
a man: no one wants to hear you whine
about your lost files.

"Database: the information you lose when your memory crashes."

Dave Barry (1947), American author

Clerk: When was the last time you backed up your work?
Carrie Bradshaw: Umm, I don't do that.
Aidan Shaw: You don't back up?
Carrie Bradshaw: No.
…
Carrie Bradshaw: Oh God Miranda, I'm freaking out, what if everything I have ever written is gone?
Miranda Hobbes: When was the last time you backed up?
Carrie Bradshaw: You know, no one talks about backing up. You've never used that expression with me before, ever, but apparently everyone is secretly running home at night and backing up their work.
Sex and the City, "My Motherboard, My Self" (2001)

iMac

I haven't lost
my mind;
I have a back-up
somewhere.

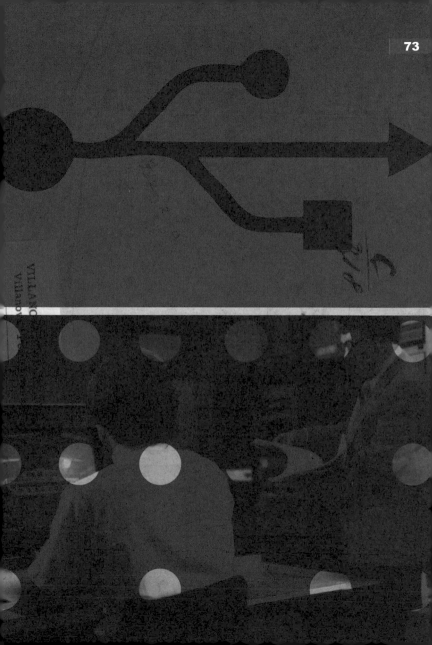

Minimize clicks

Help avoid carpal tunnel syndrome worldwide by minimizing the amount of clicks in the programs you develop or websites you design.

―――――

"We did a lot of experiments to see how many buttons the mouse should have. We tried as many as five. We settled on three. That's all we could fit. Now the three-button mouse has become standard, except for the Mac. Steve Jobs insisted on only one button."
Douglas Engelbart (1925), American inventor of the computer mouse

"I hate mice. The mouse involves you in arm motions that slow you down. I didn't want it on the Macintosh, but Jobs insisted. In those days, what he said went, good idea or not."
Jef Raskin (1943-2005), American human-computer interface expert

"It doesn't matter how many times I have to click, as long as each click is a mindless, unambiguous choice."
Steve Krug (1950), American author and usability consultant

"[A] WYSIWYG downside is that it forces too much manual labor on users and requires a stretch of imagination to envision results in advance. Yes, you can gradually massage your work into the shape you desire, one modification at a time, and visually confirm progress as you go. But you have to make each modification yourself, at the cost of many a mouse click."
Jakob Nielsen (1957), Danish usability consultant

The internet is for porn

Contrary to popular belief, the World Wide Web is more than an X-rated playground where ads for penis enlargements and webcam strippers reign supreme, although of course there's plenty of that kind of stuff floating around.

"A Mission Statement is a dense slab of words that a large organization produces when it needs to establish that its workers are not just sitting around downloading Internet porn."
Dave Barry (1947), American author

"America Online customers are upset because the company has decided to allow advertising in its chat rooms. I can see why: you've got computer sex, you can download pornography, people are making dates with 10-year-olds. Hey, what's this? A Pepsi ad? They're ruining the integrity of the Internet! "
Jay Leno (1950), American comedian and television host

"Legend has it that every new technology is first used for something related to sex or pornography. That seems to be the way of humankind."
Tim Berners-Lee (1955), British engineer often credited as the inventor of the World Wide Web

"The internet is like a big circus tent full of scary, boring creatures and pornography."
Richard 'Lowtax' Kyanka (1976), American internet personality

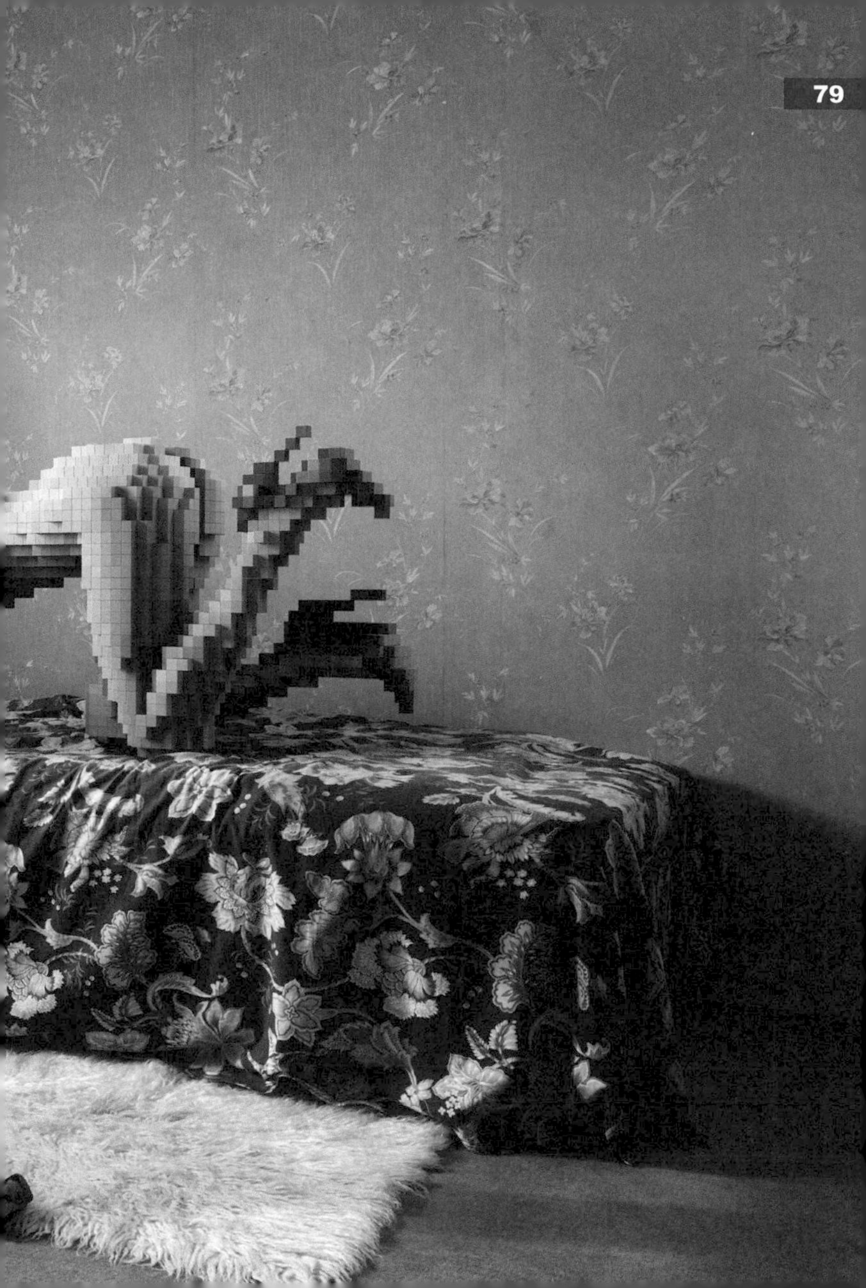

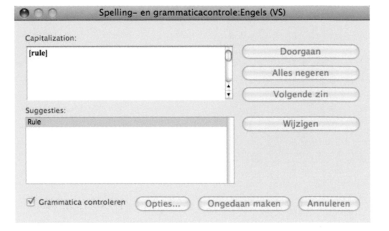

USE SPELL CHECK

For some reason emails are still regarded as a rather informal form of communication where apparently the rules of proper grammar no longer apply. Spell check is available: use it!

"Perhaps a case could be made for an email writing section to be included in English classes."
David Givens, American Director of the Center for Nonverbal Studies

"If Al Gore invented the Internet, I invented spell check."
Dan Quayle (1947), former American Vice President

"There is a big difference between poor spelling that reads as sloppiness and poor spelling that results in an entirely different word appearing from the one intended. As people have increasingly come to rely on computer spell-check programs, they've also become increasingly susceptible to creating documents where an entirely wrong, albeit correctly spelled, word has found its way into the text."
David Shipley and Will Schwalbe, American authors of Send: The Essential Guide to Email for Office and Home *(2007)*

Know thy user!

Ask any usability expert and they will tell you that you need to know your audience: the people who are buying your computer, using your software and downloading your program. So go on, get to know your users. Have them test your product. Use their feedback. And end up with something that, hopefully, is a lot more user friendly.

"Know thy user, and YOU are not thy user."
Arnold Lund, author of 'Expert Ratings of Usability Maxims', Ergonomics in Design (1997)

"Users do not care about what is inside the box, as long as the box does what they need done."
Jef Raskin (1943-2005), American human-computer interface expert

"User, n: the word computer professionals use when they mean 'idiot'."
Dave Barry (1947), American author

"Your most unhappy customers are your greatest source of learning."
Bill Gates (1955), American businessman and co-founder of Microsoft

"You can't ask customers what they want and then try to give that to them. By the time you get it built, they'll want something new."
Steve Jobs (1955), American businessman and co-founder of Apple and Pixar

"For the average project, you do not need a lab. You do not need a one-way mirror, you do not need an eye-tracking machine, you do not need five digital recorders. There's only one thing you need, which is the user."
Jakob Nielsen (1957), Danish usability consultant

"If you think your users are idiots, only idiots will use it."
Linus Torvalds (1969), Finnish software engineer

DON'T TRUST WIKIPEDIA

To dismiss all information found on Wikipedia as false would be just as ridiculous as blindly accepting everything you read on this widely-used, web-based, user-generated encyclopedia.

"Although Wikipedia has been a poster child for 'user generated content' and 'crowd-sourcing', the community-based approach has always been a means, not an end. The aim of Wikipedia is to produce a viable free encyclopedia, not just in English but in all the world's major languages. Wikipedia doesn't have to care how the work gets done, as long as it gets done for nothing."
Jack Schofield, British technology journalist

"Wikipedia is not just about looking up the interesting stuff. If its potential can be manifested, and if we can carry it forward through our organizations, Wikipedia itself, a derivative, all open for debate, it could make a huge impact because information is what matters and counts. It's going to matter more and more, and it's just a wonderful, fabulous cultural invention. That's why I keep wrestling with it."
Mitchell Kapor (1950), American software designer and founder of Lotus Development

"Wikipedia is just an incredible thing. It is fact-encirclingly huge, and it is idiosyncratic, careful, messy, funny, shocking and full of simmering controversies – and it is free, and it is fast."
Nicholson Baker (1957), American writer

"There is a constant ongoing discussion within the Wikipedia community looking at every aspect of the content to try and figure out where we can do a better job. We are always exploring issues around quality control. This includes making all the content better and more applicable to our audience."
Jimmy Wales (1966), American Internet entrepreneur and co-founder of Wikipedia

"INFORMATION ON THE INTERNET IS SUBJECT TO THE SAME RULES AND REGULATIONS AS CONVERSATION AT A BAR."

George Lundberg, American doctor and 'pioneer' of the medical internet

K.I.S.S.

(Keep it simple, stupid)

The K.I.S.S. principle is known as "Keep It Simple, Stupid", as well as "Keep It Small and Scalable", plus "Keep It Short and Simple", or "Keep It Sweet and Simple." Different names all call for the same thing: simplicity.

"Simplicity is the ultimate sophistication."
Leonardo da Vinci (1452-1519), Italian artist

"Make it simple. Make it memorable. Make it inviting to look at. Make it fun to read."
Leo Burnett (1891-1971), American advertising executive

"Simplicity is a great virtue but it requires hard work to achieve it and education to appreciate it. To make matters worse: complexity sells better."
Edsger W. Dijkstra (1930-2002), Dutch computer scientist

"Get rid of half the words on each page, then get rid of half of what's left."
Steve Krug (1950), American author and usability consultant

"We have to try to broaden the games that we develop, so that they can be played by more and more people. The key to this is simplicity, without sacrificing depth."
Peter Molyneux (1959), British game designer

"The key difference between writing for the web and writing for off-line readers is that web writing needs to be shorter."
Gerry McGovern (1962), Irish content management expert

"SOFTWARE IS LIKE SEX: IT'S BETTER WHEN IT'S FREE."

LINUS TORVALDS (1969), FINNISH SOFTWARE ENGINEER

Why buy the cow when you can get the milk for free?

―――――――

"I got bitten by the free software bug in February of 1998, around the time of the Mozilla announcement."
Andy Hertzfeld (1953), American computer programmer

"To be able to choose between proprietary software packages is to be able to choose your master. Freedom means not having a master. And in the area of computing, freedom means not using proprietary software."
Richard Matthew Stallman (1953), American computer programmer and software freedom activist

"You get the software you pay for. In every sense. To the nth degree. That's the way the world works."
Dave Winer (1955), American software developer

"When it comes to software, I much prefer free software, because I have very seldom seen a program that has worked well enough for my needs, and having sources available can be a life-saver."
Linus Torvalds (1969), Finnish software engineer

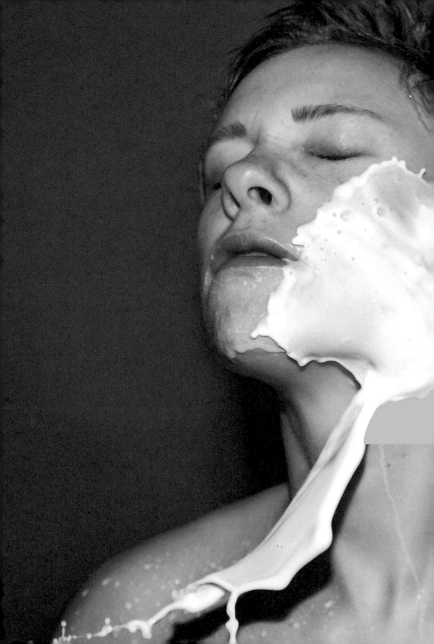

In his book, *Ogilvy on Advertising,* David Ogilvy, also known as the godfather of modern advertising, insists that white type on a black background simply doesn't work. Usability experts claim that white fonts on black computer screens work just fine. Call me stubborn, but I prefer reading my online content the Ogilvy way, with dark text on a light background.

"I am sometimes attacked for imposing 'rules'. Nothing could be further from the truth. I *hate* rules. All I do is report on how consumers react to different stimuli. I may say to a copywriter, 'Research shows that commercials with celebrities are below average in persuading people to buy products. Are you *sure* you want to use a celebrity?' Call that a *rule*? Or I may say to an art director, 'Research suggests that if you set the copy in black type on a white background, more people will read it than if you set it in white type in a black background'. A *hint*, perhaps, but scarcely a rule."
David Ogilvy (1911-1999), English-born advertising executive

"Color is an expensive luxury on paper, but comes free on the screen. Reversed type reads better on screen than it does on paper, but you should use it sparingly."
Erik Spiekermann (1947), German typographer and designer

"Use colors with high contrast between the text and the background. Optimal legibility requires black text on white background (so-called positive text). White text on a black background (negative text) is almost as good.

Although the contrast ratio is the same as for positive text, the inverted color scheme throws people off a little and slows their reading slightly. Legibility suffers much more for color schemes that make the text any lighter than pure black, especially if the background is made any darker than pure white."
Jakob Nielsen (1957), Danish usability consultant

"In printing, dropping white type out of a dark background was once a technically precarious practice. There was the danger that the thin parts of the letters would fill in. Moreover, the difficulty of reading white against black, with the vibrations that occur on the page, often proscribe printing this way."
Steven Guarnaccia and Susan Hochbaum, designers and authors of Black & White (2002)

"When reversing color out, e.g., white text on black, make sure you increase the leading, tracking and decrease your font weight. White text on a black background is a higher contrast to the opposite, so the letter forms need to be wider apart, lighter in weight and have more space between the lines."
Mark Boulton (1973), British graphic designer

Never use pop-up windows

Pop-up windows are annoying, pop-up ads downright diabolical. Despite efforts by admen to make the old pop-up ad less of an eyesore, it is still widely considered one of the most intrusive forms of online advertising. Topped only by its equally disruptive cousins: the pop-under and pop-over ads.

"I can't understand the nerve of some web users who complain about seeing a pop-up ad on our site. I give you a photo of a beautiful woman, and you bitch and moan about a stupid pop-up window? Give me a break!"
Gerard van der Leun (1945), Penthouse.com director

"Internet advertising will rapidly lose its value and its impact, for reasons that can easily be understood. Traditional advertising simply cannot be carried over to the internet, replacing full-page ads on the back of *The New York Times* or 30-second spots on the Super Bowl broadcast with pop-ups, banners, click-throughs on side bars. (…) Online advertising cannot deliver all that is asked of it. It is going to be smaller, not larger, than it is today. It cannot support all the applications and all the content we want on the internet."
Eric K. Clemons (1948), American Professor of Operations & Information Management

"I haven't spoken to any people who say 'I love pop-ups, send me more of them', but they are part of a quid pro quo. If you want to enjoy the content of a website that is free, the pop-ups come with it."
David J. Moore (1952), American online advertising executive

"If we target the right ad to the right person at the right time and they click it, we win."
Eric E. Schmidt (1955), American CEO Google

Feil

NEVER POST PRIVATE INFORMATION ONLINE

RULE
35

It never ceases to amaze just how much personal information people are willing to share. The fact that a future boss or ex-girlfriend with a vindictive streak is also sneaking a peek often seems overlooked. Would you tell a perfect stranger on the street where you live, what you're doing tonight and what you'll be wearing? Probably not, so why do it once you log on?

"Twenty years ago no one could have imagined the effects the Internet would have: entire relationships flourish, friendships prosper... There's a vast new intimacy and accidental poetry, not to mention the weirdest porn. The entire human experience seems to unveil itself like the surface of a new planet."
James Graham Ballard (1930-2009), British novelist

"My favorite thing about the Internet is that you get to go into the private world of real creeps without having to smell them."
Penn Jillette (1955), American magician, comedian and writer

"Imagine that everything you are typing is being read by the person you are applying to for your first job. Imagine that it's all going to be seen by your parents and your grandparents and your grandchildren as well. The danger is when you put something into a public space in order to share it with a few friends and in fact you've forgotten that it's actually a public space, or that the list of friends is huge, or that some of them can't be trusted not to be put it somewhere else."
Tim Berners-Lee (1955), British engineer often credited as the inventor of the World Wide Web

Don't forget the attachment!

It might seem like a no-brainer, but many an email has been sent without the proper attachment.

———

"Before you send an email laden with attachments, keep in mind the following: pack carefully and travel light."
David Shipley and Will Schwalbe, American authors of Send: The Essential Guide to Email for Office and Home *(2007)*

"Have you ever promised an attachment in your email but forgotten to attach it? What happens? Back comes a reply telling you 'no attachment' and you have to spend time resending. Take a second to double-check that your email is right the first time around."
Ian Cooper, author of How to be a Time Master: Control Your Time... Control your Life *(2009)*

THE INTERNET IS DEAD

RULE 37

The Internet has been pronounced dead many times over. Big money and big business is thought by some to have killed the spirit of the World Wide Web altogether. For now the web is still very much alive and kicking although it has definitely changed along the way...

"Major efforts are being made by the corporate owners and advertisers to shape the Internet, so that it will be mostly used for commerce, diversion and so on. Then those who wish to use it for information, political organizing and other such activities will have a harder time."
Noam Chomsky (1928), American linguist and media commentator

"The Internet? Is that thing still around?"
Homer Simpson

"When I invented the web, I didn't have to ask anyone's permission. Now, hundreds of millions of people are using it freely. I am worried that that is going end in the USA."
Tim Berners-Lee (1955), British engineer, often credited as the inventor of the World Wide Web

"The internet, the first many-to-many medium, was going to liberate us from the tyranny of centralized media and the rancid consumerism that says we are merely receptacles for what Big Business, including Big Media, wants us to buy. But the clampdown has begun. Everywhere we look, the forces of centralization and authority are finding ways to slow and, perhaps, halt altogether the advances we've made."
Dan Gillmor, American technology writer and author of We the Media: Grassroots Journalism by the People for the People *(2004)*

R.I.P.

Don't forget to play

Writing and designing computer games
is one thing, but don't forget to have
some fun along the way. Don't forget
to play.

"We don't stop playing because we grow old; we grow old because we stop playing."
Bernard Shaw (1856-1950), Irish playwright

"At the most fundamental level, 'play' has nothing to do with the competitive nature of most games. As kids, 'going outside to play' was all about doing whatever you wanted, not trying to 'win'. Sometimes the most important form of play, whether by a kid or an adult, is the simple act of messing about with something... So it is with play-testing a new game. Often, when I sit down with my group to test something new, it will just be an experiment, never intended to be a fully-playable game, but simply a piece of one."
Andrew J. Looney (1963), American game designer

"Highly successful people have a rich play life. From an evolutionary point of view, research suggests that play is a biological necessity. There is evidence that suggests the forces that initiate play lie in the ancient survival centers of the brain – the brain stem – where other anciently preserved survival capacities also reside. In other words, play is a basic biological necessity that has survived through the evolution of the brain."
Dr. Stuart Brown, author of Play: How It Shapes the Brain, Opens the Imagination and Invigorates the Soul *(2009)*

Avoid being a bandwidth bandit

Bad use of bandwidth is more than just bad manners. In a 2009 article, *Guardian* journalist Sandy Ross warns that "among IT industry experts and some environmentalists, there is concern about escalating energy demands as a result of increasing use of social networking, streaming video and bandwidth-heavy applications."

"Oxford University has added Spotify to its prohibited websites list because students were consuming so much of the university's bandwidth using the free music service."
Chris Salmon, author of "Click to download: Jukebox jury", The Guardian article (2010)

"The population of Facebook now exceeds that of America.... The software-engineering and server-farm infrastructure needed to support 350 million users burns money, and so does the bandwidth they use."
John Naughton (1946), Irish academic and journalist

"The only thing protecting the movie and TV industries from the fate that has befallen music and indeed the newspaper business is the size of the files. The immutable laws of bandwidth tell us we're just a few years away from being able to download an entire season of '24' in 24 seconds."
Bono (1960), Irish musician

"*All software sucks.*"

According to British computer programmer Alan Cox (1968), all software sucks. Apart from it being "quite hard to write software", Cox argues that, in comparison to hardware, there is less of an economic incentive to get good software out there. "The difference between hardware and software is the cost of failure. If your software doesn't work... you can ship an upgrade or a patch relatively cheaply. If someone like Intel or AMD screws up your processor... It becomes a relatively expensive operation to fix it."

"People tend to underestimate the difficulty of the task. Overconfidence explains most of the poor software that I see. Doing it right is hard work. Shortcuts lead you in the wrong direction and they often lead to disaster."
David Parnas (1941), Canadian pioneer in software engineering

"Software is usually accompanied by documentation, in the form of big fat scary manuals that nobody ever reads. In fact, for the past five years, most of the manuals shipped with software products have actually been copies of Stephen King's The Stand with new covers pasted on."
Dave Barry (1947), American author

"Software is a great combination between artistry and engineering. When you finally get done and get to appreciate what you have done, it is like a part of yourself that you've put together. I think a lot of the people here feel that way."
Bill Gates (1955), American businessman and co-founder of Microsoft

"Most software needs to be spanked."

Alan Cooper, interaction design expert

FAILURE IS ALWAYS AN OPTION

All creation is achieved by trial and error. The world of game, software and web design is no exception: failure is always an option.

———————

"Ever tried. Ever failed. No matter. Try again. Fail again. Fail better."
Samuel Beckett (1906-1989), Irish playwright, poet and writer

"As a rule, software systems do not work well until they have been used, and have failed repeatedly, in real applications."
David Parnas (1941), Canadian pioneer in software engineering

"Enjoy failure and learn from it. You can never learn from success."
James Dyson (1947), British industrial designer

"Don't worry if it doesn't work right. If everything did, you'd be out of a job."
Mosher's Law of Software Engineering

FAILURE
IS
Always
AN
OPTION

"The problem of viruses is temporary."

Back in 1988, John McAfee, computer programmer and founder of McAfee, the antivirus software and computer security company, said, "The problem of viruses is temporary and will be solved in two years." Oh irony.

"I think computer viruses should count as life. I think it says something about human nature that the only form of life we have created so far is purely destructive. We've created life in our own image."
Stephen Hawking (1942), British theoretical physicist

"In computing, as in biology, mono-cultures are bad news. They may be initially very productive, but are much more vulnerable to infection than more diverse systems. By all means get your word processor from Mr. Gates, if you must. But get your e-mail software from somewhere else."
John Naughton (1946), Irish academic and journalist

"You can't notify people by e-mail that you've given them Chlamydia. The San Francisco Health Department has a new service that lets you send an Internet greeting card to someone you may have infected with an STD: 'Roses are red, orchids are grey, congratulations, you have hepatitis A.'"
Bill Maher (1956), American comedian

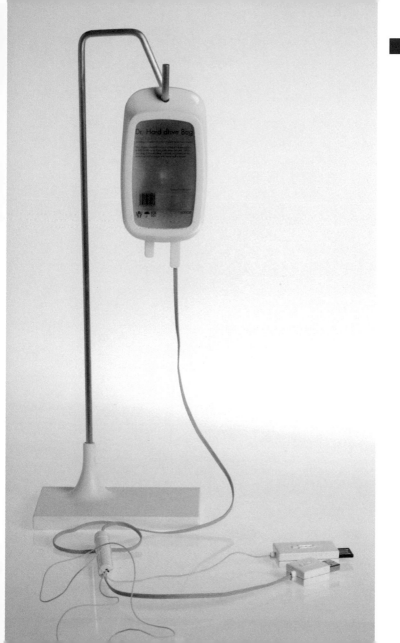

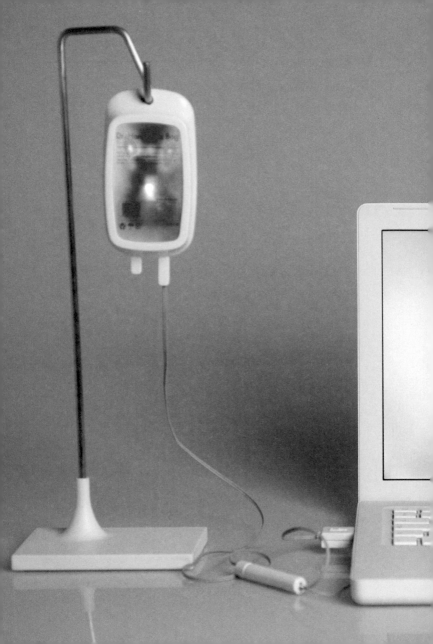

100% Recovering

MacBook

Stick to screen fonts

Because fonts that work on paper don't necessarily work on the computer screen.

——————

"If you're working on something such as a screen font, you have to get yourself into a certain frame of mind, because of the coarseness of the situation. What you're designing can never be perfect – you're not looking for a platonic ideal. You're looking at two lowercase 'e's and trying to decide which is less bad."
Matthew Carter (1937), British type designer

"Italic type on a screen is simply stupid. The pixel grid is square and does not allow for old typographic traditions. You can't make type light either, as you cannot have less than one pixel for a stroke. Go bold, go bigger, go color."
Erik Spiekermann (1947), German typographer and designer

"Times New Roman was designed for printing a newspaper, Helvetica for advertising. If you can't or won't use software that embeds your own fonts into the web page, at least use Cascading Style Sheets with fonts made for the screen, such as Verdana and Georgia, or bitmap fonts."
Erik Spiekermann (1947), German typographer and designer

"Print is a wonderful stable medium, and turns out the web is a wonderful unstable medium... Type on the web is continuously needing to be improved; over the next 2 or 3 years, at least we're going to see a lot of fonts revving and re-revving to keep up with the process."
David Berlow (1954), American type designer

"I decided to take a calligraphy   I learned about serif and sans-serif type-faces, about varying the space between different letter combinations, about what makes great typography great. It was beautiful. Historical. Artistically subtle in a way that science can't cap-ture. And I found it fascinating. None of this had any hope of any practical application in my life. But 10 years later, when we were designing the first Macintosh computer, it all came back to me. We designed it all into the Mac. It was the first computer with beautiful typography. If I had never dropped in on that single course in college, the Mac would never have multiple typefaces or proportionally spaced fonts. And since Windows just copied the Mac, it's likely that no personal computer would have them."
Steve Jobs (1955), American businessman, co-founder of Apple and Pixar

Go viral

In the world of advertising, viral marketing is the new black. Ideally, your video or campaign spreads like wildfire, deeply penetrating relevant social networks. However, it is good to keep in mind that not every cold spreads. Creating a viral doesn't always result in that much sought-after online buzz.

"Don't sell too hard. Viral means people send stuff to their friends, and no one wants to send a salesman over to a friend's house."
Chuck Porter (1945), American advertising executive

"A lot of advertising agencies are using viral marketing to try to spread messages online. Typically, they use games, corny contests, and bait-and-switch banner ads. It works; it spreads like a virus."
David Meerman Scott (1961), American marketing strategist

"Interruption or disruption as the fundamental premise of marketing no longer works. You have to create content that is interesting, useful or entertaining enough to invite. Viral is the ultimate invitation."
Jeff Hicks (1965), American advertising executive

"All viral means ... is that you've created a message that people want to share. It's proof that your message is resonating. If people want to pass it along, that's what brand marketing is all about."
Gregg Spiridellis, co-founder of JibJab digital entertainment studio

"For us, viral means a great ad. Something that someone would talk about, tell their friends about, send to them. TV spots are viral, print ads are viral, internet ads are viral when they're great."
Jeff Benjamin (1975), American advertising executive

Dramatic Chipmunk

0:02 / 0:05

Rate: ★ ★ ★ ★ ★   3,264 ratings   Views: 220,827

Always print a copy

There was a time when physically printing a copy of your files was pretty much standard practice. But it is a new dawn and a new eco-friendly day, so keeping countless hard copies on file is frowned upon. The new mantra? Think before you print. That, and keep a digital copy.

"Bring me a hard copy of the Internet so I can do some serious surfing."
Scott Adams (1957), American author and cartoonist

RULE
45

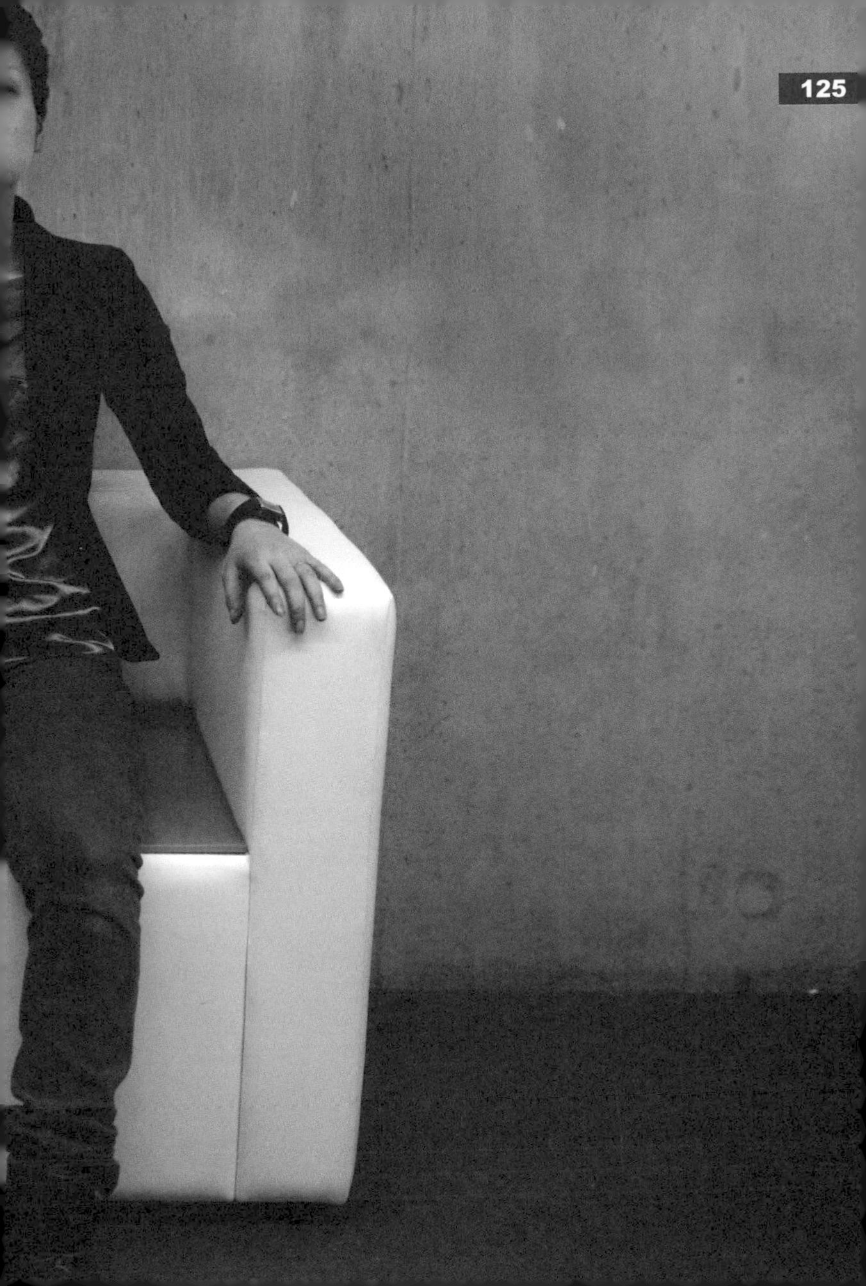

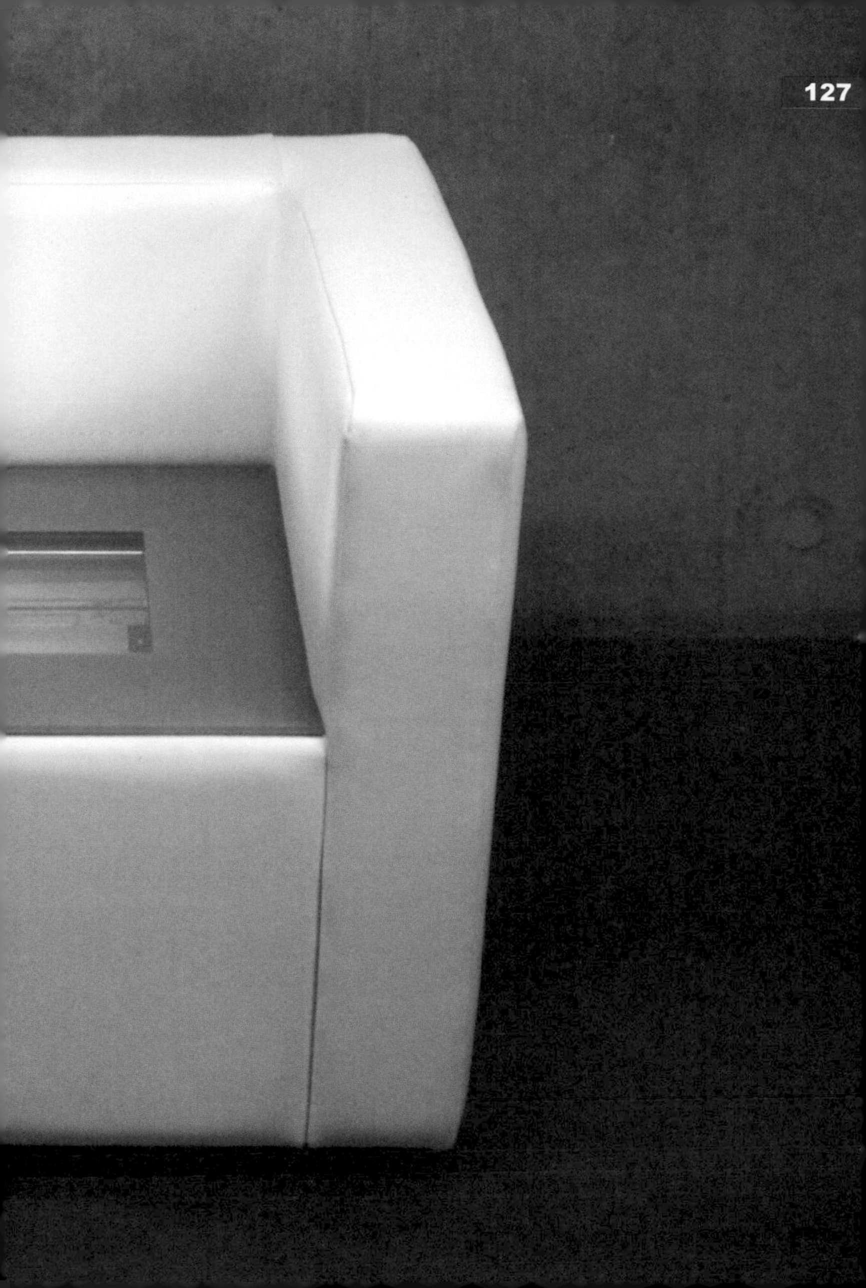

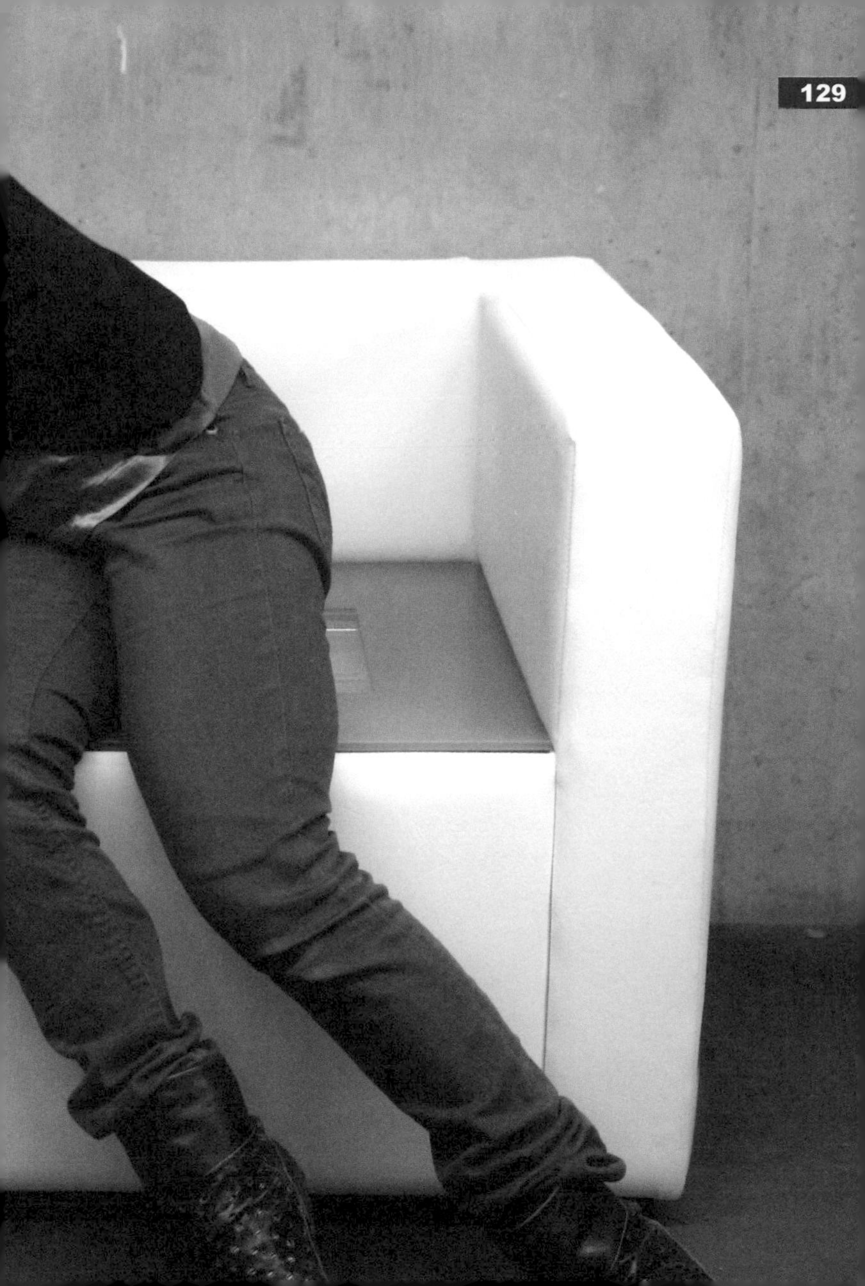

Twitter

To be or not to be followed

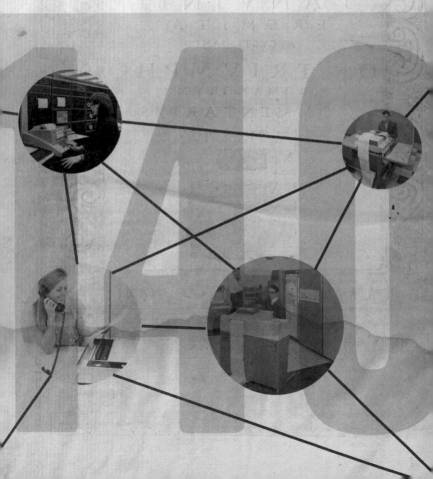

Think twice before tweeting

Just because there is technology that allows you to inform the world about every single thought you have and every intimate detail of your life doesn't mean you have to.

"A lot of serious people are using Twitter towards serious ends, especially the geeks who put it on the map. But there are also vast numbers of users, including journalists, who are so smitten with the idea of a personal broadcasting system that the absence of meaningful content to broadcast doesn't seem to concern them."
Garry Trudeau (1948), American cartoonist

"For the uninitiated, here's how Twitter works – I have no f***ing idea. I have no idea how it works – or why it is."
Jon Stewart (1962), American comedian and host of The Daily Show

"Don't forget: unlike a Facebook update, a Twitter post can be read by anyone. If you don't like the implications of this situation, either don't use the service or set your updates as protected (though this largely defeats the purpose of Twitter)."
Christopher Null (1971), American entertainment and technology writer

"I send updates a few times per day, at most. I think when people twitter 20 or 30 times per day, that's too much. They are boxing everyone else out, and people stop following them because they need a break."
Isaac "Biz" Stone (1974), American co-founder of Twitter

"Please note that re-posting something funny and pretending you dreamed it up all by your pretty little self (rather than politely Re-Tweeting), is the Twitter equivalent of buying a Mr Kipling Raspberry Swiss Roll and passing it off as your own home baking."
Laura Barton, feature writer for The Guardian

Focus first on the idea, second on the execution

After all, good ideas never go out of style, while most technology is dated by the time it hits the shelves.

———

"I would advise students to pay more attention to the fundamental ideas rather than the latest technology. The technology will be outof date before they graduate. Fundamental ideas never get out of date."
David Parnas (1941), Canadian pioneer in software engineering

"It's about trying to get results as soon as you possibly can, using things like repertoire – as in, the known, the familiar, the practiced, the repeatable. Use any tools you've used before, any code you've used before, any frameworks you've used before; because getting the results is the most important thing. You've got to get shit happening – you can talk about it, you can write it down, it means nothing until you actually make it and think f**k that's nothing like what I thought it was going to be! That happens most of the time."
Gary Penn (1966), British game developer

Log off

Step away from the computer every
now and then. No one likes a recluse,
let alone being one.

"Why do people keep insisting that I
join the twenty-first century? I live in
the twenty-first century! I just don't
want to be bothered by the shitheads on
the Internet!"
*Harlan Jay Ellison (1934), American
author*

"The Net is a waste of time, and that's
exactly what's right about it."
*William Gibson (1948), American
science fiction author*

"No one ever said on their deathbed,
'Gee, I wish I had spent more time
alone with my computer'."
*Dani Bunten Berry (1949-1998),
American game designer*

"I have no life, just e-mail."
*Michael Jantze (1962), American
comic strip writer*

GeT a Life

WYSIWYG

Sorry but WYSI(not always)WYG…

"Tablets are not bad for a skilled artist – there is a human touch that a tablet fulfills better. In the real human world we reach with our hands to objects we want to touch or move. It's a bit unnatural to reach in a direction and have the effect take place elsewhere. It is kind of a violation of WYSIWYG."
Steve Wozniak (1950), American computer engineer

"The name WYSIWYG came about during a visit from Citibank representatives. We had a demo showing how we could display a memo with nice fonts, and specifically the Xerox logo in its specific Xerox font, on screen, and then send it through the Ethernet and print it out on the laser printer. So we printed what we had created on the screen onto transparent slide stock. Part of the demo was to push the button to print and then we held the printed version up, in front of the screen, so you could see through the transparent stock that the two were identical. Actually they weren't exactly identical, but they were close enough. It was pretty impressive. One of these visitors said, 'I see, what you see is what you get.' Which was, of course, you must remember, the Flip Wilson tag-line from Laugh-In, which was a big TV hit at the time. I think he was doing a female impersonation. What you see is what you get. Well, that's the first time I heard it used around the system, which was the first incorporation of that idea, so somehow the term WYSIWYG must have spread from that event."

Charles Simonyi (1948), Hungarian-American computer software executive and developer of Bravo, the world´s first WYSIWYG editor

Computers aren't for voting

RULE
50

Bill Maher, the American comedian who called for the 'Reply All' button to be moved farther away from the 'Reply' button (see Rule #20), also favors the paper over the electronic ballot. "Voting by computer sounds really cool and futuristic – if this were 1969! But now that we all have computers, we know that they are, in fact, huge fuck-up machines. (...) You thought the 2000 election was bad? Wait until the next one is decided by a customer-service rep in New Delhi."

"E-voting systems actually provide less accountability, poorer reliability and greater opportunity for fraud than traditional methods. People assume that electronic voting is just the same as other technologies we use in everyday life, like banking or airline ticketing, but there are crucial differences. With all these other systems there is a physical data trail, bits of paper that allow us to check that the transactions are accurate. E-voting offers none of these safeguards."

Dr. Rebecca Mercuri (1954),
American computer security expert

"It is commonly said that insanity is doing the same thing over and over again while expecting different results. Yet this is what we keep doing with electronic voting machines – find flaws and try again."
Wendy M. Grossman (1954), American journalist

"Before a society entrusts its central democratic process to machines, it ought to take reasonable steps to instill public confidence in the technology. This requires only two very basic provisions: all machines must leave a paper trail that can be independently audited after the election; and software used in voting machines must be open to public scrutiny to allow any interested party to examine it and find bugs, which can then be corrected."
John Naughton (1946), Irish academic and journalist

Break the rules

Read all 50 ridiculous web rules? Now you know them, feel free to break them.

———

"Computers are like Old Testament gods; lots of rules and no mercy."
Joseph Campbell (1904-1987), American lecturer and writer

"Rules are overrated. They need to be changed by every generation. That is your most important mandate: if it's not broken, break it."
Richard Serra (1939), American sculptor and video artist

"Rules are good. Break them."
Tibor Kalman (1949-1999), Hungarian-born American graphic designer

"Game design up to now has been about making rules."
Hideo Kojima (1963), Japanese video game designer

CONTRIBUTORS

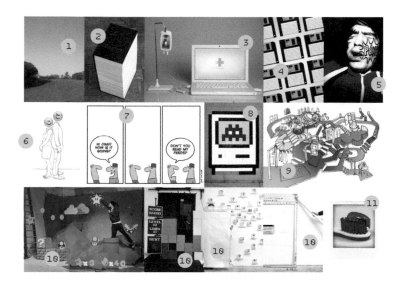

1 Fabian Rodriguez (cc)
(www.flickr.com/magicfab)

2 Rob Matthews
(www.rob-matthews.com)

3 Hyuh Jin Lee
(www.hyuhjinlee.com)

4 Julian Kleyn (cc)
(www.flickr.com/juliankleyn)

5 Jason Rogers (cc)
(www.flickr.com/restlessglobetrotter)

6 miss-tal
(www.miss-tal.com)
Link to the full strip:
www.miss-tal.com/heart-story.html

7 Oliver Widder (cc)
(http://geekandpoke.typepad.com)

8 Stefan Kloo (cc)
(http://www.flickr.com/lord-jim)

9 Florine Kammerer
(www.vollmondtag.de)

10 PIXELGARTEN
(www.pixelgarten.de)

11 Ellie (cc)
(www.flickr.com/ella_marie)

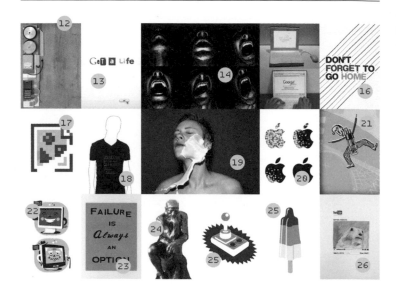

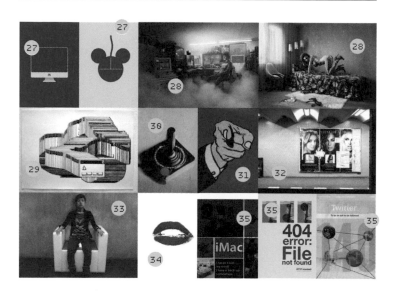

27 Rodrigo Müller
(www.flickr.com/rodrigomuller)

28 Jean-Yves Lemoigne
(www.jeanyveslemoigne.com)

29 Petter Buhagen
(www.petterbuhagen.com)

30 Paul Downey (cc)
(http://blog.whatfettle.com)

31 Nick J Webb (cc)
(www.flickr.com/nickwebb)

32 David Ben Gourion
(www.flickr.com/epoxy_one)

33 Tomomi Sayuda
(www.tomomisayuda.com)

34 geishaboy500 / THOR (cc)
(www.flickr.com/geishaboy500)

35 Rétrofuturs (Hulk4598) / Stéphane Massa-Bidal
(www.retrofuturs.com)

INDEX BY NAME

Also available

Never Use White Type on a Black Background
And 50 other Ridiculous Design Rules

"One of the most fun and quirky books one can read about rules in the world of fashion and design. Great for a laugh and to challenge your thinking and pre-conceptions as a designer."
- *Design Indaba Magazine*

ISBN 978 90 6369 207 0

Never Leave the House Naked
And 50 other Ridiculous Fashion Rules

"The book is neatly designed. Small format, great graphics and plenty of illustrations commissioned to talented young graphic designers."
- *We Make Money Not Art*

ISBN 978 90 6369 214 8

The Medium is the Message
And 50 other Ridiculous Advertising Rules

"The book light-heartedly pokes fun at statements that, either for good or bad, have become clichéd principles of advertising."
- *Dezeen*

ISBN 978 90 6369 215 5

Never Use More Than Two Different Typefaces
And 50 other Ridiculous Typography Rules

ISBN 978 90 6369 216 2
Publication date: September 2010

BISPUBLISHERS
www.bispublishers.nl

Thanks to:
Premsela, Dutch Platform for Design and Fashion (www.premsela.org)
Lemon scented tea (www.lemonscentedtea.com)